The Glorious Summer

TONI ORRILL

Hamilton Books
A member of
The Rowman & Littlefield Publishing Group
Lanham • Boulder • New York • Toronto • Plymouth, UK

Copyright © 2007 by
Hamilton Books
4501 Forbes Boulevard
Suite 200
Lanham, Maryland 20706
Hamilton Books Acquisitions Department (301) 459-3366

Estover Road
Plymouth PL6 7PY
United Kingdom

All rights reserved
Printed in the United States of America
British Library Cataloging in Publication Information Available

Library of Congress Control Number: 2007932300
ISBN-13: 978-0-7618-3797-8 (paperback : alk. paper)
ISBN-10: 0-7618-3797-3 (paperback : alk. paper)

Front Cover: Oil on Canvas by Michelle Koeppel
Photograph by Sally Dunn

∞™ The paper used in this publication meets the minimum
requirements of American National Standard for
Information Sciences—Permanence of Paper for
Printed Library Materials,
ANSI Z39.48—1984

To Ellis and Jack
Treasures of My Heart

My Maker, My Husband
I am forever your grateful vessel and humble servant
2005

In Appreciation Of

The Editorial Review Board of University Press of America
The Rowman & Littlefield Publishing Group, Inc.

The assistance and dedication of Acquisitions Editor:
Patti D. Belcher of Hamilton Books

The time and energy of my personal editor:
Susan Davis of London, England

The support and insights of my artistic friends:
Michelle Koeppel of New Orleans and Colman DeKay of Los Angeles

These angels for their friendship and fellowship:

Kimberly Cross of Tampa, Florida, Dedra Faine of Washington, D.C.,
Dr. and Mrs. Felix Mathieu, Jr. of Houma, Louisiana; Laura DeCastro
(In Memoriam), Sandra Fuentes, Nicole Pailet Gentry, June Joseph,
Angela Lang, Joa Montana, Miss Jimmie Oleaga, and Amy Reggio

All friends and neighbors of New Orleans, Louisiana

These women of God who have guided and inspired my faith:

The Reverend Dr. Sherry Adams
My Stephen Minister Ellen Jones
St. Paul's Episcopal Church, New Orleans, Louisiana

The forevermore friendship and love of A. T. Jenkins
The amazing soul and magnificent spirit of daughter Andrea Jenkins
The prayerful encouragement of Pastor Jonathan Ziegler
All of Covington, Louisiana

My family and grandparents—
Lester G. Muller (In Memoriam)
Mrs. Lester Muller of Oldsmar, Florida

Contents

Introduction	vii
The Tale I Tell from New Orleans	1
Swimming	5
Galaxy	9
Domino	11
Eternity	13
Glowing	17
Rain	21
Halo	25
South Shore of Lake Pontchartrain	27
Drifting	29
Wildflowers on the Fourth	33

CONTENTS

Soaring to Upstate New York	35
Mosaic in Saratoga Springs	37
Rose and Rock at Yaddo Gardens	41
Farmington in Folsom	45
Moccasins of Mandeville	49
Kismet in Covington	51

Introduction

I am no one by admission, unqualified, just an ordinary soul earnestly intent to try the purpose of pain, offer opportunity out of loss, and tell of a time when all hope was hidden, life sparse, a magical city unaware of the groundswell of future tragedy.

If expression is a form of joy—mine has no training, only the sincere desire to inspire after deliverance, send the compelling message dwelling within this mind's complexity.

How I ever ended up here or there I am indeed uncertain, for I was never an author, this tome far from a book but scribbled thoughts recorded in a simple black diary during an extraordinary season of 2005.

As I complete the story today from a sleepy town on the Atlantic coast, I sit with great disbelief that the intense moments of transformative soul-searching

INTRODUCTION

and personal suffering documented then would now be publicly understood, found of interest to anyone other than my own psyche.

Only in retrospect does one comprehend life exposed and naturally flawed, passionate, vulnerable, deep in dark more than light. The loss of perfection—a family undone—seemed almost unbearable in those days. I still remember every ounce of grief as though time was turned.

One can never view the entrance without finding the exit door first, and as much as I believed after penning the last chapter the worst of sadness had arrived, a far more harrowing saga struck.

Several entries of this book were written in New Orleans before Hurricane Katrina—the fearsome bookmark survivors use to delineate their memories and segregate their life stories.

It is worth mentioning the contextual landscape to truly understand the journey before you, to see with proper perspective human control as true fiction, destiny as divine ruler of unimaginable circumstances.

In the months following, this piece was far from realization, saved in a hard drive awaiting its cue to emerge in an appropriate environment.

INTRODUCTION

It was actually my collection of essays written after the historic storm, titled *The Broken Fall*, that uncovered the following pages of this natural prelude to its unnatural sequel.

The courage to seek publishing was followed by many offers of rejection, then a miracle moved, and way cleared for this opening you now begin.

I cannot adequately project its worth or value, however if one counts grace, I pray you discover this lesson a priceless gift of faith.

Toni Orrill
Cocoa Beach, Florida
February 2007

The Tale I Tell from New Orleans

The brass lock set into place. Unlike myself, it is the perfect fit to its mate. I also realize that nothing echoes louder in an empty house than goodbye.

For the first time in nine years, I am completely alone, no longer able to hide in wifedom and motherhood. The boys are off to sleep away camp, my husband estranged one month ago.

I could always count on my mate to fill the lulls of busyness, but he left as urgently as he descended upon my world, and unexpected change was knocking hard and fast as I closed the door on a marriage and chapters of child-raising.

That story is the perfect opera for a rainy day, but the universe is not cooperating on this brilliant June morning, and it is difficult to work with the stars in daylight.

THE TALE I TELL FROM NEW ORLEANS

The energy required to unveil this tale I tell was spent last night combing the corridor, a restless, anxious spirit of delicate Swiss dot and worn slippers.

By daybreak I realize I am no longer a young lady with ideas and ideals, but a wanting woman, too close to forty for comfort, buried beneath laundry, activities and obligation, overtaxed by private schools, church, charity, not to mention a family with many extensions.

I am honored to have made a success of every one of their goals; and the sacrifices required for their accomplishments—the projects shelved for a spouse's work, the sleep broken when a child needs a nurse, the hours at doctor's offices understanding the aging mind's loss.

Did God perhaps hear, in all his divine wisdom, these groanings, recognize dreams that somewhere along this path of familiarity became muffled, then eventually silent?

I have had little time or inclination to associate with this soul speaking today. Like a sorority sister, we are forever connected but greatly out of touch.

Four weeks alone together was a confounding idea, the most unwanted proposition, like the awkward expectation of an uninvited guest who determines to be my best companion.

Left with no choice, I fumble into the pool of emotion, adrift but with the hope and fear of reconciliation and restoration, to find her.

Swimming

What started as a very difficult morning evolved into an afternoon of strength by sheer mercy. After a flood of tears, I realize that so many of my fears are well warranted from childhood, protectively hidden in the past. A quiet treasure chest of rejection and chaos, a box I rarely have courage to delve into, but whose contents escape and antagonize my decisions, marriage and esteem decades later.

While I am aware on the surface that these strongholds have been erased by a merciful God, I am always unprepared when these mistakes erupt to distort my carefully managed mirage of wholeness and self-confidence.

Each day, I see a glaring image in the pool, my crystal reflection, high above on the board from which I warily bounce, wondering will the net of water take shape to catch my pride and fear, buoying me up from the depths to the oxygen-filled world my lungs fervently need to sustain?

I am exercising each day, all the while discovering how blessed I am to move with symmetry, to travel from here to there by commanding my body to coordinate its parts in search of the deep end. I flip and stroke to the other side, moving efficiently and freely toward my next goal.

This "deep-end" morning taught me much about the value of distance. A symbiotic friend of healing—healing of the heart—distance creates perspective and too often, I have abandoned my own salvation in the wake of a drowning loved one. Unable to merely offer a hand, I leap overboard to rescue, and need the safety of solid ground to steady my legs and clear the deck.

As long as I guarded the lives of others, I could never disappoint Him with my own iniquities. Perhaps this feeling of isolation is simply a God-given opportunity for self-reflection and spiritual growth. As the wise father, He has untangled our mess, separating our souls to surface for air. Individually, I fear, my performance may not win His golden ribbon.

SWIMMING

In truth, His standards are not equivalent to His perfect value—for how could I ever offer Him what does not belong to our world? Instead, we enter a fluid process as we advance the spiritual rungs, much like the art of swimming. Becoming more "Christ-like" is not simply walking in His ways, but butterflying in His faith without a clear, definable goal—a ladder, a mother's arms or the deep-end to reach.

The ultimate goal is to keep riding waves of hope through the interference to know and love Him even more. That, I have discovered today, is all our great instructor requires.

Galaxy

It only takes a single shooting star to remind us of the brevity of connection, how briefly scent lingers after a departure—a flight foreshadowed only by prescient periwinkle eyes knowing that it is only a single unilateral move away from the sum of which it no longer desires to be part of.

Each night, this wavering wonder, uncertain of his precise solo destination, contemplates an impending launch date while his constellation, a fragile lot of dots and dashes, anxiously fears when the glorious picture of a unified existence will officially collapse into an incomplete sky graphic.

I have never understood the difference between a comet and a shooting star, their divine natures, composures and dispositions. Are they equally powerful and radiant, just distant enough to travel in the same galaxy, but never to really cross paths? Or are they entirely different personalities of irreconcilable differences?

What makes a shooting star shoot? Burnout? Boredom? The burning need for escape? Or rather, is it just flighty, compelled to explore a deeper galaxy, and too unhappy to fuel its current world?

Witnessing a shooting star is undoubtedly a godly experience—a memorable sight in a lifetime. Yet one rarely considers the dust left in its path, a trail of shattered crystal remnants, broken by its burst into the unknown—a village of bright sparks, left-behinds, lacking wisdom of its whereabouts, comings and goings.

If only that one star would be a reliable and sustainable energy, like older suns, complacent and content in stellar surroundings—instead of the type burst by a calling to the unknown.

There are never new endings, just beginnings. We reposition our lives into fresh formations, confident we are able to outshine our source of warmth.

Instead of drawing closer towards our eternal flame—an inexhaustible giver of life—we strive to hang our own moon, and go it alone in the darkness. Tonight I will gaze into His brilliant power and know that He, and only He, is God.

Domino

Mornings are quite anxious—overwhelmed by the unknown and crazed with poor decisions. These days, I am not sure where I will even live, fall into place, now that my home is broken by design.

But in the blessing of a single day—one that dawned as ordinary—those moments of doubt too have passed, and my fears are cleared by an impossible pattern of mercy stilling all movement until I praise His name.

While my ivory tower has tumbled before His patient eyes, His plan is stamped in black-and-white, unmoving, never-changing, just a steady smooth road of hope that human error cannot misplace.

To live in that peace, to melt into perfect will, to surrender this broken soul amazes this mind with grace.

DOMINO

I *am* numbered, spotted by the Lord, and despite all feelings of earthly independence, have been given the right to face the day as a solitaire, or accept the invitation to be half of His pair.

While the temptation to stack my tiles of life according to my own understanding is alluring, to align my will with His plan, I have found today, is my single chance of victory.

For all of my control, or lack thereof, and futile attempts to piece this life together, cannot remove the domino keeping His love in order.

Each square houses mystery and logic, and I now accept God's help to build my love up towards Him instead of sideways towards man—peacefully accepting His hand to steady mine with trust.

I did not separate the covenant God connected, and now, must simply hold my space, a frightened dark spot, frozen within the rectangle of His light.

All of my tactical mistakes cannot blind His perfect sight nor undo His perfect game plan. I simply continue to play like a child, knowing my luck is just beginning to change.

Eternity

I wait and pray for God to speak, act, to appear—to untie the knots of this tangle—but His glorious message is disguised or completely absent today. To be still and know He is God, omnipotent and sure, that He has not cut loose these heartstrings, nor snipped my frayed edges into peaceful form—only tightened the circle of uncertainty I long to unravel.

My angel of patience is en route as I wrestle through boredom, hoping to receive the one fruit of the spirit I have yet to sample, the worst virtue He could have chosen for me to reckon with.

I am a bull ready for salvation, a burst of movement—to sprint through this pen of quiet activity toward a happier pasture, run with rhythm instead of fighting the silence of eternity.

Yet, each hour of pain ushers in another hour of intimacy, a long loop of hope that one day, His glorious plan will understand these questions and myself discern the answers.

He is methodically moving the light of my sun, the moon out of direction with the same degree of time, I am certain, required to hang the stars and dust the beaches. If only I can appreciate both of His hands, large and small, instead of favoring the stronger.

I await God, actively disguised, working out the infinite seconds to complete His masterpiece—timeless and steady—while secretly simmering with expectation, arrival, a deep understanding of these supernatural events that erased my life in one divine sweep.

The voice of heaven must be worth this wait, a call louder than a sonic boom, but I hear only chimes of wisdom, randomly blown by the occasional breeze, instead of the clanging bells of sturdy towers.

Be still and know I am God, I repeat, but this restless soul needs a predictable word, a sign of time, a gentle glimpse of the reward this pain will bring in the not-too-distant future. When will this inexhaustible moment heal and be made whole again? When is eternity?

I respectfully seek the date and time, then turn face and reset my dial.

The truth reminds me that only He could ever hold the hands of time so responsibly, strike them with such precision, that a chaotic world revolves with order, fashioning synchronicity to arrive exactly on time—never a minute late or a second early.

My faith is now learning to pace itself, once eager, now humbled to obey that power of perfection of which neither my speed nor haste could ever locate single-handedly.

It is a journey I have committed to, destination unknown.

Glowing

From a restful state I feel a sweet morning call, like the uneven whispers of an eager child on holiday, anticipation brimming in each excited breath, a hush impossible to contain.

I secretly wonder why He is moving at such an unusual hour, interrupting the magical movie now paused by this mind, fascinated with possibility.

My shadow follows His lead to discover a burst of glory revealed—once the dense coal of a smoldering night—now a watercolor so absorbing, nothing this day brings could unravel its artful peace—the glorious momentum of daybreak, a morning born of darkness.

Divine opportunities to witness natural beauty rarely grace a span of time; it billows through the open window, a slow silent wave missed only by a quick glance in an earthly direction.

GLOWING

I, myself, stand content to admire existence from the other side.

He places the canvas on its proper pedestal, as I record this event here, for the grand unveiling set to a chirping ensemble of tree frogs, a gathering of robins. So bountiful is the serene luster of His glowing backdrop that language is rendered irrelevant—if only one listens for His call within the blank slate of slumber!

What beauty stored overnight and how faithfully installed before the regal arrival of the sky lion, piercing the dove-like monotones with stinging darts of fire.

When one truly honors the overture and finale of day, showstoppers between the blind and the fruitless, then the soul truly recognizes a living God.

As the orchestra of creatures carries His tune, life grows small, the delight of a God on earth, well-versed in the details of our minds, incredibly powerful.

And if He has shared such formidable energy to nudge the globe into daylight, we can be most assured that He moves equally through every angle of our conscious world, way past midnight, well before morning breaks.

GLOWING

I remain in the dress circle of His fast-paced, drizzling second act. A moody sky stretches into peaceful positions as I succumb easily to His invitation of the day. Dramatic drums of clashing air force me to curl up with His word, while spheres of raw light plant me stationary to hear the falling concerto of the heavens.

For the sunlit yesterday, seeds grounded for the fruits they will bear, has passed, my dry heart thankful for the gift of weather, a drop of rain.

Rain

The wet manna obediently pours from looming grey ghosts to the ground. Like the early dew, I come to understand how to follow, never to question, but to simply oblige.

Without a plan or control of conditions, the need to know the score and plan my shot no longer at my mind's disposal, I am now as relieved as a dutiful Indian to the powers that be.

On the receiving end of instruction, one discovers great self-discipline—humility to accept another's choices, focus to act and fortitude to accomplish.

The afternoon is raining peace—to simply accept and respond to His plan instead of questioning intent and examining strategy.

Drops are called by name, indeed named by their call, relinquishing any and all desire to serve, never curious for the reason of this day or when the random moment will come to water a thirsty land with the blessing of moisture.

Nor do they question the size or shape He chooses, content with their appearance, not coveting the strength of ice or the unique intricacy of a flake of snow. I catch a piece of His wisdom from the sky, opening wide to accept truth and beauty in an equally graceful manner.

Authentically-crafted and gloriously free, our identities, souls, the very hairs on our heads, like the pebbles at my feet, are generously crafted, intimately nurtured, and drawn into constitution.

On this balmy evening of summer, the giver of life is watering creation, offering a drink to creatures near and below, washing away the uncertainty of why I am chosen to be in this moment, at this writing desk.

The words on these very pages are overflowing streams of His consciousness, His touch on every key. I, an unworthy drop of pain, have become His vessel. A calling I am not directing, but simply believing as summer showers.

RAIN

Imagine, like the elongated fronds of palm, absorbing this falling gift graciously and thankfully. For it is simply not its tender nature to turn away from the source of life but instead, to stand tall, silent and grateful—accepting soothing provision to quench its parched spirit.

No longer will I await sunny skies for picnics or minted snow for angels, but rather to view the gift of a day from a thankful heart instead of through a looking glass of expectation.

Halo

Amidst two Christians peace is near, close to perhaps possible, even should only one prefer to patch the pain while a brother ignores the gap of forgiveness. Tonight, in a rare moment of grace, my husband and I broke bread to seal the past and plod towards agreement.

We are unusual enemies, in love and out of time, fighting a boundary closed by decisions, dictated by the swollen ambiance of the table shared, dialogue deafened only by my heartbeat, by which our beloved reason for this meeting became life.

A gift of angels cherished nowadays by our armies of anger each hoping to place a flag in his hostaged halo.

To win is to heal, the melting of ice still clinging to the half-empty glass, cautiously seeping pride into understanding, calming fire into truth. Despite all discord, someone we love, a child of God, sits wounded and hurting for a truce.

To inherit the earth, we must call the mighty weapon we wield to its knees, spot the flare of a ship shouldered, like a sparkler on a stranded beach.

A silent war of sorts, myself poised and praying for the candlelight to soothe the uneasy limbo of emotional hunger, to burn words into bridges of glory.

How conflict arises I am unsure, but I recognize the smoke fainting into soiled air, the oil of the lamp cold and used now, a room dangerously clouded with dull laughter, the friendless mess of plates piled, clamoring to close the meal.

I treasure this shrapnel from the fallout—a settlement founded, the branch of peace offered before the rainbow of midnight.

South Shore of Lake Pontchartrain

After hard-to-sleep nights and angst-filled days, today God the Giver wanted me to bask in the beauty of the natural world. Joy is the ultimate blessing, so rather than submerge myself in worry, I have turned my troubles over to Him, depositing them with great relief in His sanctuary of freedom.

Mentally, this level of trust in the wilderness is childlike and arduous, considering the enemy is pressing hard on my courage, the fear of self-destruction surrounded by validation. I stand alone in this fight, my will hobbling towards shelter, spirit dizzy, helpless to ever know victory without the miracle of intervention.

Release is a difficult concept—requiring bold faith that He is willing and capable of handling all affairs as the soul sojourns from the issues of the day. While my head fought for control this morning, my heart followed a paramour toward the lake to absorb His calm power.

Through all of His might, He captured the water, protecting it with a rocky rim of sand and shore to nurture life forms invisible and enormous one's feet need simply to touch a single soft grain to rejoice.

My head swims with newfound pleasure, arms caress the warm rush of love.

How insignificant one feels when the sky drinks the sea, when a crash of watery strength interrupts the crowd of stillness. Yet we are drawn to the beach of life to restore and refresh our bodies—feeling with each sweep and break, that He is unquestionably the stronger of we two.

In this space, one has air to breathe far beyond the invisible horizon, as He guides apparitions of tiny triangles with a single breath, skimming and dipping them until they arrive safely to the anchor of dry land.

In the calmness of days such as this, peace glows, my lips bow, body balances on strong golden hands. A gaze mountain steady, fingers opened, frame twisted with each brackish sway.

For hours, I will accept this escape at the shore of the city.

Drifting

Sleep comes during the waking hours, restlessness throughout dark ones, the timing confused—never right and regular, much like the world in which my soul now rambles—drifting on a plateau of promise, ready for the spare stalks to melt into pink buds of pleasure.

I yearn for sheer happy moments that ripple my insides into bellows, gestures not rejected but embraced, genuine consolation received in lieu of cautious pity—glorious delight that stretches knots of anguish into the fine embellishment adorning a lily-white dress.

When do these tangled moments weave into joy, the mountain moved to unveil life cast ashore during this voyage of pain? I long to feel the joy as deeply as I know the sorrow.

DRIFTING

This night of concern is not rare, but all too comfortable in its tattered dressing, despair cleverly suffocated in a pillow's ear. It began hours ago with a single call of friendship. The how-are-yous rather not received. Only I understand this vulnerability is not a point of discussion, but a gutless soft spot shy of inquiry, pleased to churn and toss alone.

Life these days is unfathomably complex, promises crushed by selfishness, imperfect roses ripped from their stems. I strive to hold onto the invincible pain that, despite its thorny edges, is mine, and these cuts I choose not to share for reasons that are personal and intimate.

They remind me of a man escaping difficulty for possession, ownership of a love that twisted and distorted my notion of pure intent.

Still, the well meaning continue to call, somehow believing their reticent offers can relieve this unbearable hole of wanting of all I have ever known, dreams I continue to outstare.

My disappointment begs for release, fretfulness searches for freedom, a resting space of resolution. Until that time of mercy, trust must be found in the arms of an invisible stranger whose unconditional love I forget to remember.

Fate may have brought me to His door of consolation, but faith has pushed me through an illuminated passage where ransomed fear is exchanged for priceless protection.

Trust in the Lord with all the heart, who uses, never creates, these unkind conditions that wreck our wondrous worlds until they are roughly recognizable to call by name.

I turn to Him to remind me I am beloved, chosen, precious and dear without the gilded strands of friendship and spinning web of social circles.

Behind the scrim of shadows, I hear His voice, the perfect husband I know as my maker, and I rest in hope without calamity.

Wildflowers on the Fourth

Freedom is a gift, as I am reminded of this holiday morning by the wildflowers growing along my path, His everlasting arms wrapped around the random earth.

To see God live, winding up the massive oak, the weeds wandering without value, full of resiliency to allow the harshest of rejections—never to be chosen—is indeed reason to celebrate. My heart declares happiness in the steamy sun of July.

I have now grown accustomed to blessings ringing at my feet, the gleaming optimism of pompons, the spell I cast on their cottony tops, a salutation to singlehood.

I stir the sample plucked, a happy dancer centered by spangles of orange, still moving as my hand stops its tambourine. An awkward seed, it has yet to grow into its curvy green stem, the long-grained banner it nicely crowns.

Its past—told by each weave of its stalk—a search for amber waves, a stumbling of spirit into love of the country grass. His promise, the pursuit of a shiny new creed of make-believe, I am ready in a minute to pursue.

To glide by, glancing into the face of liberty, is revolutionary for myself personally. While His majesties shine, I now know life independent of man, having released this tarnished crown of captivity into a brass band of harmony.

As the streaks scratch the black board with smoky tails of joy, freedom is found, His grace shed upon all.

I am devouring the pie, blowing trinkets of glee, knowing now I belong only to me. A day of revelry, I stand alone with authenticity.

Soaring to Upstate New York

A summer here at home, a damp winter there, the clash of nature wills a dismal gulf into high seas of drama.

There are flights of fright destined to be part of this fateful course of self-discovery—elusive enough never to be predicted by the simplicity of minds such as mine. I am at the mercy of the weather, again, out of control of circumstance.

One day ago, at this precise moment, I weathered a truly physical storm—one that only He has the technical nature to stir. It was the first real test of this marriage in the making—Would I trust him enough to make these sheets of weather into a hidden bed of comfort?

He first sent an irresistible angel, and a rare lull in the whirlwind of dusting doom, to let me know that I am no longer a survivor without a shipmate.

SOARING TO UPSTATE NEW YORK

After long moments of modern inconvenience came the unveiling of romance from a tiny torch glowing in the warmth of beeswax.

To absorb Eros, one must never expect its bountiful course, nor pencil its poetic threat, but to simply allow its desire to come from its own striking heart through the pores of a lover, the petals of peonies.

I am shaken still to plan my escape and embrace His faithful rescue.

With colored wings aglow, I soar for safety, away from the loving catastrophe after the passionate calm. He is traveling with me, crafting wings for the bluebird to fly.

I arrive in scanty shape to make a day of sightseeing, resting finally near still waters, a moon of honey sparkling on the Northern lights, my rich provision dwelling in a small inn until daybreak.

No return flight do I require, knowing only the wistful longing for my beau, an apple draping the blown trees, ripe in the city fled.

Mosaic in Saratoga Springs

This soul has always been attracted to the old, places sturdy and true to their roots, where divinity is not distant, but swells our imagination with spirited air.

My eyes gaze upon a wondrous nestling of beech bestowed by deep, ground-breaking hands into this ridge of beauty—a rare, linear stock that never sways nor cowers in the harshness of life, shielding their tender young with downy coats until their souls slowly measure each passing winter.

When the season is nigh, they shed their cloaks for a dressing more suitable for the company of those, like me, migrating to their foothills on a journey to upstate New York.

Yesterday, I admired a living portrait of American history, as I meandered through practical towns and vintage forts, en route to an enclave my children have been blessed to appreciate for a small summer.

I was greeted by a strong gapped grin, smiling my services away. In just two weeks and missing teeth ago, my lanky grade-schooler has become a thoroughbred, competing on the camp course to own the winner's circle of life—of which the trophy is not mine for the taking. I am honorably dismissed from duty during this month of milestones.

God had been preparing me for this still photograph my heart must take—a reality no mother can respectably bear—a job undone, an empty nest becoming a successful one, the twist of purpose into a confused self.

In this lake town, time is on our side, the missing half not slept on since pregnancy, now turned toward a wall of complacency instead of a mate.

My sentiments were shared by many on that disheartening ford, while kisses of honesty were blown from bare faces, eyes full of misty moments on the back roads home.

Nature teaches our hearts quiet acceptance, namely the venerable families at the cabin door, who have trained up their seeds to prosper far beyond all they ever imagined and desired.

I monitor their maternal presence, admiring the wisdom lovingly stored in hearty chests, branches open and kind, mingled carefully with younger saplings, content in evergreen.

Graceful arches are built-in sparingly, screened by scalloped leaves and straight pins for protection.

A coal-feathered crow flits from camp to camp. I hear her loving instruction and concern. She, like the maple, is training up her young, tagging His word around their feathered necks, confident their promise to fly with valor will come true.

Inspired by this enchanted forest, I rest in their shades of legacy, drinking in the springs of healing.

Rose and Rock at Yaddo Gardens

A single white aspen greets a Gothic retreat on the eastern edge of Saratoga Springs. The wrought iron gate speaks, "Bind My Love."

I am mesmerized by the endurance of the etching as dusk tumbles the tiered wedding cake into quarters of fountains, placid statues and rows of rose and rock.

South of the windowed manse rests a watery tribute of enduring affection, a platinum well of tears poured from a wife adored, utopia mourned into pleasures forevermore.

The marble bench, from which I perch, uses its mature eyes to watch this eternal sandglass of romance resist the weeping firs of evening. I study the family unknown yet trusted in stone, like the wheat of alabaster placed beneath the pines.

ROSE AND ROCK AT YADDO GARDENS

From this distant spot, I spy the dream keeper, his cape captured in the imaginary Adirondack wind, boots still shined in honor of the bridegroom, fist fast in protection of four young lost. He understands that home is wherever God chooses to dwell, in the nonsense of grief and the grove of love.

I, too, stroke a broken locket of gift and curse, hear the genius composition of highs and lows, flowing from the velveteen ground below. What control a garden offers to those who tend its flowers and grapes, preserving their growth as a poem or prose.

For each hand is entitled to a hole for digging, man and wife equal angles of love to cement or adorn—His an island of rugged release, Hers a pergola of translucent pearls on its way to paradise.

I meet her beauty unexpectedly, frozen in an immortal face, fear that her headdress is mine, bewildered and blue, hardened with hope that life again will blossom into expression, a gift cherished into one shared.

The trickling stream slows at the muse amongst cherry queens and tamed ferns, strengthening again along the trail of lace and bamboo, towards a shrine of solitude.

ROSE AND ROCK AT YADDO GARDENS

And there his pain stands as obedient as the vow of a perfect heart. When she awakes, he is still with her, and without this love, they were indeed nothing.

Farmington in Folsom

Things are not always as they seem, situations are only as true as our eyes explain.

Tonight, I move towards a private piece of God's territory north of the city skyline, my vision bridled by the pitch of night.

Courage is found in the country, trust a way of life. I myself am comforted more by the rush of activity than the speed of wilderness, the solace of a horse's rhythm.

My longtime friends and gracious hosts are at home in this stable of passion, my heart surprised by the joy I have missed in their welcoming faces. Where they lodge, I will lodge for the weekend, amidst ponies and fruit stands, posted fences and open land.

Without the spark of a firefly, senses circle this blind pathway, wrapping an extraordinary farmhouse in a blanket of groomed fields and loquacious streams.

My foot gripping the last step of comfort, I am blindingly aware of my vulnerability, as deep as the ink-stained landscape I wander in search of concealed trust.

Unlike the creatures of this night, I am not at home, as close to the south shore as I am to the certainty that this shaky ground is indeed worth taming—and not a natural border to a dangerous descent.

My loyal companion remains on the porch, head poised with concern for this senseless call for partnership—a polite request he alertly obeys. With my guide at my feet, I dare this moment noir, surrendering to its silent cave of straw stalactites dangling by the gentle grace of fig.

The windows are shuttered by absence, lamps covered with baskets of willow. We listen for directions toward a place where tall shadows never slumber, the spirituality of knowing mares abounds.

The stream speaks kindly as we settle at its flowing foot, all hesitancy rocked away by His loving sway of a roped crib, suspended by humidity and pine legs, canopied by the silhouettes of hickory.

We find that His peace of the night is a dark, special blessing reserved for those who ride into the other side of light.

Moccasins of Mandeville

The only glimpse of that memory named joy is a place I am driven to, called to, because there, my lonely world is one with His refuge.

In this hamlet of artistry, a new season is within sight, where nature and grace grow hand in hand, where I long to discover the rarity of quaintness instead of the common grounds of the cityscape.

One can see the pink and periwinkle welcome sign 30-miles out, the luminous and gentle coastline, the calmer and quieter of the two lakefronts. I now favor the company of the one who listens more than speaks, who lures a story without raising a single question.

On her side of the family land, misshapen rust and alabaster prod my moccasins, abundance swirls my spirits like the pelican's flight above.

MOCCASINS OF MANDEVILLE

The greeting of the natural world is powerfully simple, if only one accepts its handshake of peace.

Tonight, an unknown prince there awaits beauty, where among authentic fare and friends—He has prepared a table for two—two uncertain if they will ever find one.

I warily leap the line dividing my life, across the wide lanes that bridge the sister landings, leaving behind the shiny packages along the busier bank. The garland, strung for miles with clustered globes, fades from vision.

I am ready to move, to be planted like a tree by the river, to inherit this land and dwell upon it forever.

Kismet in Covington

The rambling wooden cottage disappears in its own clothes, waiting humbly like an orphan for a family to match its hard-to-find beauty. Asleep, its peaceful pose awakens our dreams to live again in a place we call home.

It is true He sees its needs, hears our hearts, and finds the miracle of acceptance in those knowing only abandonment.

On this late-morning excursion we meet our Maker, my Husband, to find salvation in each line and lever of this rustic temple's kismet bones.

Weeks ago, I could only envision the nimble little feet, dancing their tense tendons into the grains along the eastern end of the wooded landscape, pray to inherit this land and never be moved.

Anchoring its thorny heart is a bamboo grove protecting the beachy cove of a slow rolling waterway.

On this small private shore at the edge of overgrown acres, our children innately understand that they belong in the very vines and berries clinging to their fair ankles.

My brave, handsome warriors work the raw space, patch bridges of logs, dip the depth of swimming holes, and rebuke the artificial lives their natural souls steer through each day on their calls of duties. Like the troops of tadpoles, our family knows only this moment in time.

We are blissfully beat by refreshment, pleasure so pristine and subtle—cypress nooks, fishing hooks and honeycombs of queens—that, if happiness could live only for these hours, our last supper would undoubtedly be a picnic on the rocky organic bends of His promised land by the bogue.

www.ingramcontent.com/pod-product-compliance
Lightning Source LLC
Chambersburg PA
CBHW031555300426
44111CB00006BA/329